Scary Creatures

WOLVES

Written by
Penny Clarke

Illustrated by
Bob Hersey

BOOK HOUSE

Created and designed by
David Salariya

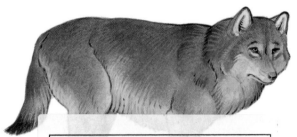

Author:

Penny Clarke is an author and editor specialising in information books for children. The books she has written include titles on natural history, rainforests and volcanoes, as well as others on different periods of history. She lives and works in Norfolk.

Artist:

Bob Hersey has worked in many mediums, including designing 3-dimensional models, artwork for advertising and illustrating children's books. He lives in Sevenoaks, Kent.

Additional artists:

Carolyn Scrace
David Stewart

Series creator:

David Salariya was born in Dundee, Scotland. In 1989 he established The Salariya Book Company. He has illustrated a wide range of books and has created many new series for publishers in the UK and overseas. He lives in Brighton with his wife, illustrator Shirley Willis, and their son.

Consultant:

Dr Gerald Legg holds a doctorate in zoology from Manchester University. He worked in west Africa for several years as a lecturer and rainforest researcher. His current position is biologist at the Booth Museum of Natural History in Brighton.

Editor: Karen Barker Smith

Picture research: Matt Packer

Photographic credits:

Aflo/naturepl.com: 24
Anthony Crane Collection, UK/Bridgeman Art Library: 27
Martin Harvey/NHPA: 11, 17
Kitchin & Hurst/NHPA: 6
Getty Images: 4, 22
International Sheepdog News: 25t
Mountain High Maps/©1993 Digital Wisdom Inc: 28-29
Lynda Richardson/CORBIS: 25b
Andy Rouse/NHPA: 19
Galen Rowell/CORBIS: 18

Every effort has been made to trace copyright holders. The Salariya Book Company apologises for any unintentional omissions and would be pleased, in such cases, to add an acknowledgement in future editions.

Published in Great Britain in 2004 by Book House, an imprint of
The Salariya Book Company Ltd
25 Marlborough Place, Brighton BN1 1UB

Visit the Salariya Book Company at
www.salariya.com
www.book-house.co.uk

A catalogue record for this book is available from the British Library.

ISBN 1 904642 24 1

Printed in China.

Printed on paper from sustainable forests.

Contents

What is a wolf?

A wolf looks like a German shepherd dog. Or does the dog look like the wolf? That is more likely because wolves are dogs' ancestors. Wolves eat meat, so they are carnivores, like dogs. Female wolves produce milk to feed their cubs, so they are mammals, also like dogs. Wolves usually live in family groups, called packs. But if food is scarce they will live and hunt alone.

Wolves living in less snowy areas often have darker coats

Wolves live in the northern hemisphere from the Arctic and Siberia in the north to Mexico, Spain and the Middle East in the south. They have evolved different coats according to where they live. In the cold north wolves have very thick coats, but in the south, where summers are long and very hot, wolves have thinner, smooth coats.

Is this a dog or a wolf?

This is a dog, a Siberian husky.

Many centuries ago, the native peoples of the cold northern regions domesticated the wolf. They developed strong, tough breeds of dog, including the Siberian husky, to pull their sledges for them.

Did you know?

In many parts of the world wolves are in danger because the forests in which they live are being cut down so roads and towns can be built.

Wolves living in snowy regions have paler coats than those living where there is little winter snow (left). In snowy regions a dark coat will allow prey to quickly spot the wolf, making hunting difficult.

Why are wolves scary?

Wolves rarely attack humans, so why are we afraid of them? They are big, strong and are excellent hunters, often working as a team to track their prey. They hunt at night and can move silently across their territory. Perhaps the most scary thing about wolves is their howl. It's a wild, haunting sound that can be heard through the night.

X-Ray Vision

Hold the page opposite up to the light and see what's inside a wolf's head.

See what's inside

A snarling wolf is certainly scary, but few humans will ever see a sight like this (right) in the wild. This image shows why wolves are such efficient killers – look at those teeth!

How do wolves communicate?

A lone wolf howls to find out if other wolves are nearby. A pack will howl to tell other packs to keep off their territory. Scientists believe wolves also howl because they enjoy it.

Wolves communicate by howling.

6 North American grey wolf, or timber wolf, howling

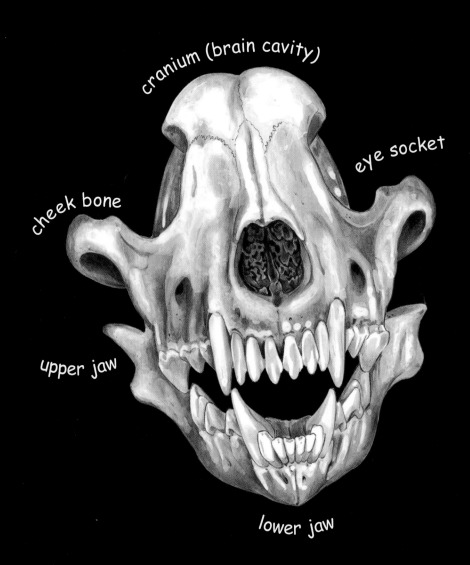

cranium (brain cavity)

eye socket

cheek bone

upper jaw

lower jaw

Skull of a wolf (front view)

Are wolves killers?

Wolves are carnivores, which means they eat meat as their main source of food. The wolves of Alaska, north-west Canada and southern Iraq also eat fish. All wolves have the strong jaws and teeth which carnivores need to cut through the muscles and crush the bones of their prey.

Did you know?

A large male wolf can eat 9 kg of meat at one meal. The alpha (dominant) wolves in each pack always eat first.

Wolves use their large canine teeth to hold prey and tear through muscle. The carnassial teeth cut through the meat when the wolf is eating its kill.

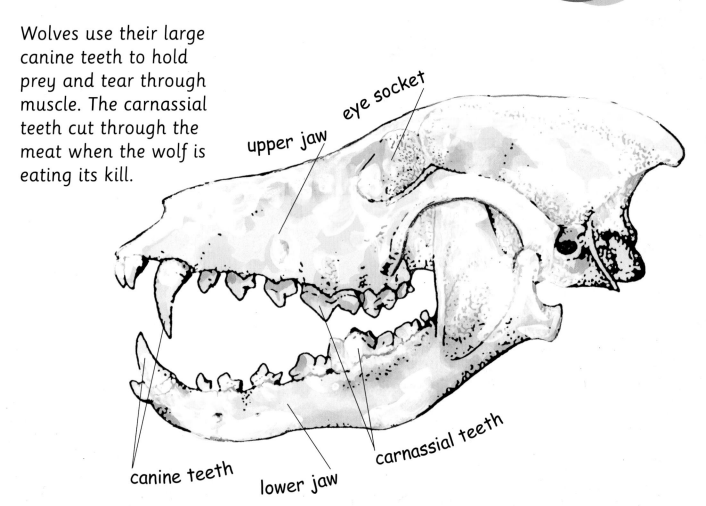

Skull of a wolf (side view)

Submissive wolf

How do wolves live?

Wolves are very social animals and usually live in family groups called packs. Each pack is headed by an alpha male and female. These two wolves are usually the strongest and the parents of the other wolves in the pack. The alpha wolves dominate the others, who behave submissively towards them. The alpha wolves always eat first, the rest of the pack waiting until the alphas signal that they too can eat.

Dominant wolf

Top: A junior wolf shows submissiveness with half-closed eyes, laid-back ears and closed mouth. Above: The normal expression of an alpha, or dominant, wolf.

How is each pack organised?

Like puppies, wolf cubs romp and play. However, these 'games' are serious, helping to establish which cubs are bigger and stronger. This will influence their position in the pack when they become adults. Each wolf knows its position and behaves accordingly.

Every pack has a strict order of rank.

senior wolf

lower-ranking wolf

When two wolves meet, the lower-ranking wolf crouches, tucks its tail between its legs and lays its ears back (above).

Ethiopian wolf group

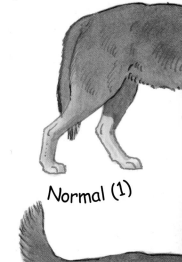

Normal (1)

Self-defence (2)

Complete
submission (3)

Did you know?

Wolves are pack animals, but in areas where they are threatened and food is scarce, they have adapted to living alone. They regroup when they have cubs.

What do tails tell?

The position of a wolf's tail depends on the animal's rank in the pack. Normally a wolf's tail is relaxed and hanging down (1). A high-ranking wolf's tail is raised and stiff when it meets another wolf, showing self-defence (2). Complete submission is shown by a limp tail hanging between the legs (3).

The lower-ranking wolf lies on the ground and licks the senior wolf's nose and face (above).

Finally, if the senior wolf still seems aggressive, the junior rolls on its back, showing it is completely defenceless and poses no threat (above).

11

How do wolves hunt?

Wolves usually hunt in a pack. However, if there are no large prey, wolves hunt alone or in pairs. Where they hunt large animals living in herds, such as buffaloes or elk, pack hunting is essential. Wolves will stalk the herd, often for several days.

X-Ray Vision

Hold the page opposite up to the light and see what's inside a wolf.

See what's inside

Working together as a pack

When the alpha male gives the signal, the pack attacks, separating a weak animal from the herd. It is often the younger female wolves who do this job because they are lighter and faster. The heavier male wolves bring the prey down.

Chasing prey

If a pack separates a healthy animal from a herd by mistake the wolves soon stop chasing it. Chasing an animal they know they can't catch is a waste of energy.

Surrounding the prey

Buffaloes are much too big for one wolf to tackle (left). When a pack attacks, the buffaloes surround their calves and weaker animals. The wolves circle this protective ring, snapping and snarling, trying to break through it. When they succeed, the pack rushes into the centre to attack a calf.

Pack of wolves attacking a buffalo

Did you know?

Wolves travel great distances at a steady 8-9 kph. They can reach 56 kph, but only for short bursts when hunting. Reindeer, important prey for wolves living in Arctic regions, can reach 64 kph.

skull

chest vertebrae

spine vertebrae

ribs

tail bones

Did you know?

Wolves, like all animals that travel long distances, have big, strong leg bones. These big bones will support the strong muscles that wolves need.

What's inside a wolf?

All wolves have strong, muscular bodies, but they vary in size. Northern wolves can weigh up to 54 kg. They need large bodies to survive winter temperatures as low as –30°C. The pale desert wolf seldom weighs more than about 18 kg. Its lighter body helps it survive summer temperatures over 30°C. Northern wolves could not survive in the south and their southern cousins could not survive in the north.

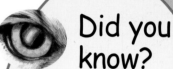

Did you know?

When a wolf pack hunts in deep snow, each wolf walks in the footprints already made by the alpha leader. This saves energy that they will need for chasing their prey.

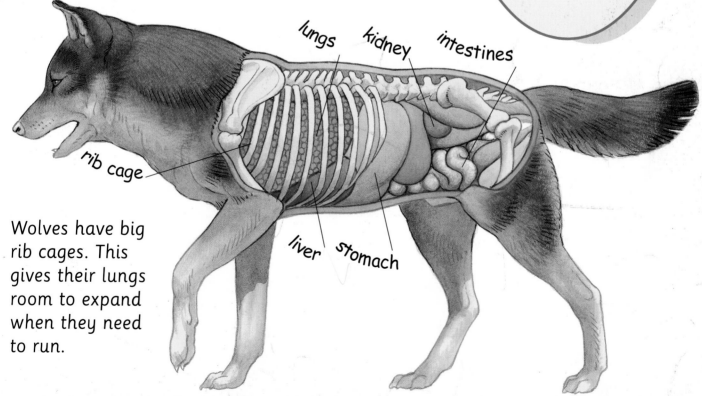

Wolves have big rib cages. This gives their lungs room to expand when they need to run.

lungs kidney intestines

rib cage

liver stomach

Cutaway of a wolf, showing some of its internal organs

What do wolves eat?

What wolves eat depends on where they live. Wolves in the cold north eat large animals, such as reindeer, elk and musk-oxen, as well as rabbits. Some packs also catch fish: when salmon come upriver to breed, the wolves flip them out of the water with their paws.

In warmer areas there are fewer large prey and wolves eat mice, rabbits, birds and even frogs. Sometimes they attack flocks of sheep and foxes. All wolves will occasionally eat fruit and berries.

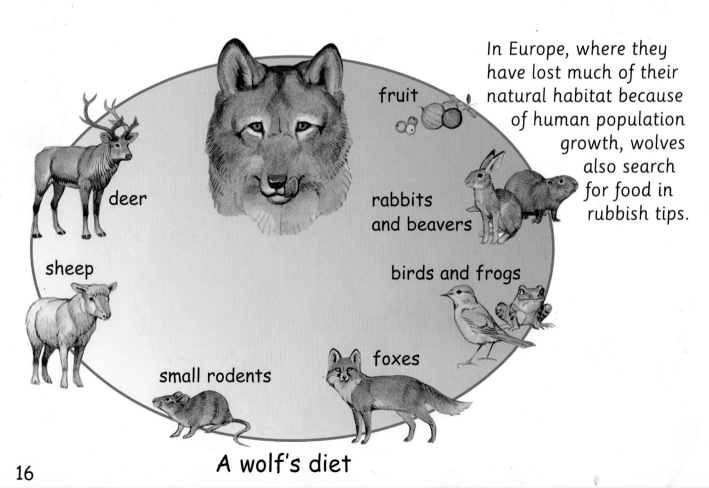

fruit

In Europe, where they have lost much of their natural habitat because of human population growth, wolves also search for food in rubbish tips.

rabbits and beavers

deer

birds and frogs

sheep

foxes

small rodents

A wolf's diet

Ethiopian wolf mother with her cub

Did you know?

Female wolves suckle their cubs for between six and nine weeks. Then the cubs eat partly digested meat the adults regurgitate for them.

Do wolves have enemies?

People are wolves' greatest enemy. In past centuries, when there were fewer people, there was more space for wolves. Also, at that time hunters only had low-powered weapons with which to hunt wolves. Today, growing towns and cities are destroying wolves' natural habitat. Modern-day hunters use high-powered rifles with night-sights, so wolves have little chance of escaping.

Wolf-skin hood

The Inuit people of the cold north traditionally wear wolf skins for warmth (above). In the past, hunting for a family's needs kept the wolf population in check but did not threaten it. Today, most hunting is just for sport and some types of wolf have become endangered.

Why do people hunt wolves?

Wolves will sometimes attack domestic animals, such as cows and sheep. Over the centuries, farmers in some areas where wolves are common have bred special dogs to protect their livestock. Laying traps to catch wolves also used to be common but is now outlawed in many places. A wolf caught in a trap like this (right) could take many days to die.

People hunt wolves to protect livestock or just for sport.

jaws of the trap, closed as they would be around a wolf's leg

pressure plate

A wolf trap

Did you know?

Wolves are being reintroduced into parts of the USA. Many were wiped out in these areas in the early 20th century.

Arctic wolf in the snow

Is it a wolf?

All over the world there are animals that look similar to wolves, but they are not wolves. Scientists believe many of these species descend from the same wolf-like animal that lived millions of years ago.

Is this a wolf?

No, it is a Tasmanian tiger.

The Tasmanian tiger, also known as the marsupial wolf or thylacine, is a large carnivorous marsupial. It lived on the Australian island of Tasmania, but was hunted to extinction by the end of the 1930s.

Coyote

Dhole

The coyote lives in North America in many of the same areas as the wolf. It is smaller and is often called the prairie wolf.

The dhole is also called the Asiatic red wolf. Dholes live and hunt in packs from southern Siberia to Sumatra and Java.

African hunting dog

Did you know?

Wolves live only in the northern hemisphere, but wild dogs live in all parts of the world except Antarctica. Like wolves, they are all carnivores.

African hunting dogs live on the savannahs, or grasslands, of southern Africa. They hunt in packs and are extremely fierce – even lions and leopards avoid them.

Maned wolf

The maned wolf lives on the grasslands, or pampas, of South America, from Brazil to northern Argentina. It hunts in marshland and around lake edges, catching animals and water birds.

Fox

Dingo

As many European foxes now live in towns and cities as in the countryside. Scavenging rubbish bins for food is easier than hunting!

When settlers reached Australia several thousand years ago some of the dogs they brought with them escaped. They developed into today's wild dingoes.

How did a killer become a pet?

Scientists believe that about 10,000 years ago wolves became the first animals tamed by humans. No one knows exactly how it happened. Perhaps hunters killed a female wolf and took her cubs. Or an injured wolf, unable to hunt, hung around a human settlement, scavenging food. Gradually it may have been accepted by the human group – just another pack to the wolf.

Many dogs no longer look like their wolf ancestors, but they still lie in this relaxed, but watchful, way (above).

Did you know?

Wolves trot more often than they walk. When they are trotting each stride covers about a metre, but this increases to 1.5 m when they are running very fast.

Why do people and dogs get on so well?

Humans and wolves both discovered advantages to living together. The wolf got a regular supply of food without the effort of hunting. It also got shelter and the warmth of a fire. Humans got a guard dog and an animal that helped them hunt better. They both gained a companion. People and dogs still benefit from the relationship today.

Humans learned to make use of the way wolves hunt and circle their prey. Today's sheepdogs are doing what their ancestors did, but now they obey the human shepherd as their pack leader and herd the animals instead of going for a kill (right).

Sheepdog herding sheep

Spaniel howling

Wolves howl to communicate with each other, but dogs don't. Occasionally a dog will howl (left), perhaps in response to something on the television or to music. The howling may be caused by the sound of another dog or animal, or a high frequency sound that human ears cannot hear.

A wolf pack is led by an alpha wolf. A pack of trained hunting hounds (right) always has one or two experienced 'lead' hounds.

Who's afraid of the big bad wolf?

Wolves rarely attack people. However, many myths have developed with wolves as villains, showing how much people have feared them. The saying 'keeping the wolf from the door', meaning to keep hunger away, links the wolf with hunger as something to fear and avoid.

Sometimes wolves are not the villains. In the ancient Roman legend of Romulus and Remus, a wolf fed the twins with her milk (above) when their wicked uncle abandoned them. The story goes that later, Romulus founded Rome (the capital of Italy) in the place where the wolf had discovered them.

Are werewolves real?

Stories of werewolves, mythical creatures part man and part wolf, are common in northern Europe. In the past these fearful creatures were blamed for anything that went wrong, such as bad weather, poor harvests, dying cattle or family disasters.

Artist's impression of a werewolf

No, werewolves are mythical creatures.

19th-century fairy-tale illustration of the wolf meeting Little Red Riding Hood

In the days when dense forests covered much of Europe and North America there were few roads and people did not travel far. They were more likely to be attacked by robbers than wolves but the wolf's reputation for fierceness and cunning led to many stories about the terrors facing travellers. The wolf is the villain in the tale of Little Red Riding Hood, who travelled through the forest to visit her grandmother.

Wolves around the world

Wolves live only in the northern hemisphere, from the cold of the Arctic to the heat of Saudi Arabia and southern Mexico.

All wolves are closely related, but there are different types of wolf. Scientists call them subspecies and there are 23 varieties in all. These wolves have evolved so they can survive the climates of the regions where they live. Large wolves with thick coats live in cold regions, while wolves living in hot areas are much smaller and slimmer.

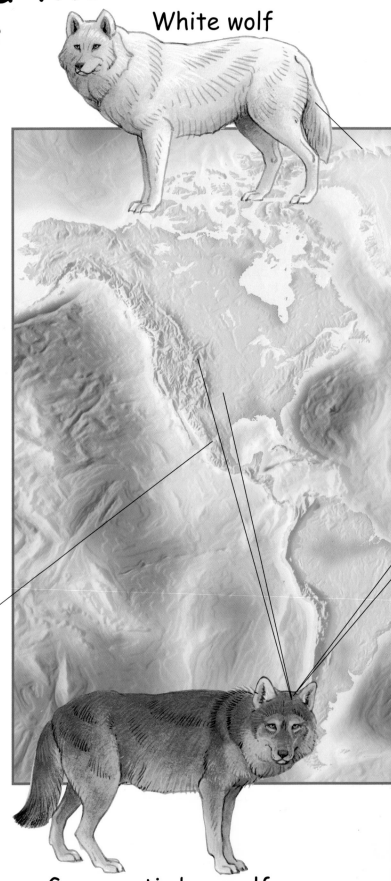

White wolf

Grey, or timber wolf

Mexican wolf

Brown wolf

In Europe most wolves live in the east, especially in Poland. Some still survive in Germany, Italy, Spain, Portugal, Greece and former Yugoslavia. There are also a few in Scandinavia.

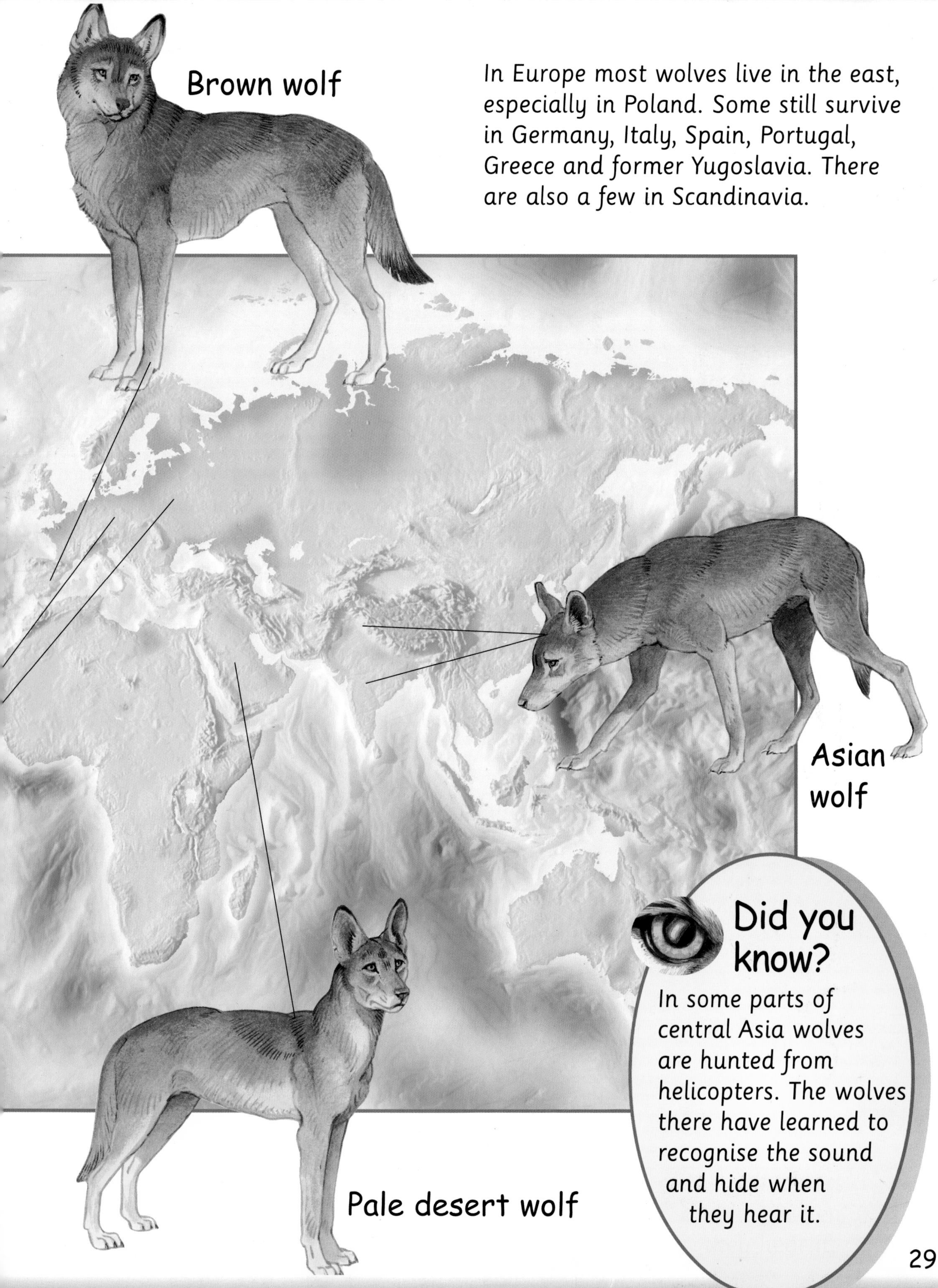

Asian wolf

Pale desert wolf

Did you know?

In some parts of central Asia wolves are hunted from helicopters. The wolves there have learned to recognise the sound and hide when they hear it.

29

Wolf facts

Wolves used to live in Britain but had been exterminated in England and Wales by the 16th century.

The Vikings, who terrorised Britain and the coasts of north-west Europe from the 8th to 10th centuries, were nicknamed sea-wolves because they were so fierce.

Only the alpha male and female wolves in a pack breed. The other wolves help raise the cubs. For the first few weeks the female stays with her cubs to feed them and keep them warm. Because she cannot hunt, the pack members bring her food, leaving it at the entrance to the den.

The size of a pack's territory depends on how much food there is. The more food available, the smaller the territory a pack needs.

The last wolf on the Falkland Islands was killed in 1876. The wolves were so tame (like most animals on the islands), that they were easy prey for fur hunters.

By killing weak individuals, wolves help keep herds of animals, such as reindeer, healthy. In places where wolves have been wiped out, the reindeer herds become too large. There is not enough food for them all so many die of starvation.

In Bulgaria there are only about 100 wolves left – the rest have been killed. However, jackals have moved in to the region and now kill more farm animals each year than wolves ever did.

In central Asia farmers' crops are being damaged by huge numbers of rats and mice. The wolves and foxes which ate them have been hunted almost to extinction.

Wolves in Russia are said to have learned a new trick: if they are being chased by hunters in a vehicle, they move across to the driver's side. This means the passenger with the gun cannot see to shoot the wolf, so the driver has to do a U-turn. This gives the wolf a chance to escape.

In the Second World War (1939-45) groups of German U-boats (submarines) that hunted and destroyed many Allied ships were nicknamed 'wolf-packs'.

Glossary

adapted Something that is suitable for a particular purpose.

alpha Term describing the most powerful wolf and the leader of the pack. Each pack usually has an alpha male and an alpha female.

ancestors An early type of animal from which a later type has evolved.

carnivore Animal that eats the flesh of other animals as its main source of food.

communicate To exchange ideas by certain behaviour.

domesticated An animal that can be kept under control or that is adapted to living alongside humans.

dominate To control or rule over someone or something.

endangered Animals that are few in numbers and may be close to extinction.

environment The surroundings where an animal lives.

evolve To develop gradually over thousands or millions of years. Through evolution animals become better suited to their environment.

extinct Species of animal (or plant) that is no longer alive anywhere in the world.

habitat The particular environment where an animal lives.

mammal An animal that feeds on its mother's milk when it is a baby.

marsupial Group of mammals in which the females carry their babies in a pouch.

prey Any animal that is hunted by other animals for food.

regurgitate To bring up food that has already been swallowed.

species A group of living things that look alike, behave in the same way and can interbreed.

submissive To allow yourself to be dominated by someone.

subspecies A group of animals in a species that is slightly different from the rest of the species. This is usually because the animals of the subspecies have been isolated from the rest of the species for a long time or they live in different conditions, for example the wolves that live in northern Canada and those that live in India.

suckle Feeding a young animal, like a wolf cub, on milk from its mother's teats.

territory An area controlled by an animal or group of animals.

Index